I Hate Sex, But…

I Hate Sex, But…

By June E. Whitehorn

iUniverse, Inc.
New York Lincoln Shanghai

I Hate Sex, But...

iUniverse, Inc.

For information address:
iUniverse, Inc.
2021 Pine Lake Road, Suite 100
Lincoln, NE 68512
www.iuniverse.com

ISBN: 0-595-31892-4

Printed in the United States of America

To my sister, Julia, who helped me through thick and thin with this book;
In loving memory of Anthony Kacir;
And to Cliff Taylor, the one, the only.

And I can't forget Stephanie Zipay and Karrissa Hill, with whom I have
laughed outrageously about bloopers and sexual mishaps.

Contents

Author's Note

Way back in the day, like around 1994, I used to write lists about everything, ranging from what I hated about life, to what I hated about cars. I had a bunch of lists. There wasn't one thing in this world that I couldn't complain about. And what better thing to complain about than sex? I mean, let's face it: nobody complains about sex (other than the fact that they might not be getting any). Well, I came up with a few things about sex (among other things) that I just can't stand. You know what I'm talking about: the sloppiness, the wet spots, the unprecedented gas. Then there's stuff about men, the weird things that we women just can't seem to figure out. There's also stuff about women that we women hate. Now, mind you, none of this is in any order, so number one on the list isn't necessarily number one. Everyone seems to think that important things are at the top, but they're not. We all hate things, and we hate so many of them, it's honestly hard to put a number one on anything. But, to balance it out, I also threw in a lot of the things that we, as human beings, love about sex and men. It's funny, I honestly thought I hated more about sex than I loved, but once you find that right person, it's hard to keep hating it. This book got really hard to write these last couple years.

So, without further ado, I'm going to let you loose on some pretty embarrassing stuff. A lot of this stuff happened to me, and that which didn't happened, to someone else. This is meant to laugh at, to giggle about, to think about. It's fun. It's simple. It's my book. I really hope you like this.

A Few Things
I Hate about Sex

Some time ago, I was sitting in my art class back in high school thinking about how terrible my sexual experience the night before had been. Thinking about it just made me upset, so I decided to talk to my friends—more like the whole class—about sex.

"I wonder why everyone seems to think that sex is so wonderful," I began.

One guy turned to me and shook his head pitifully. "Maybe you should just kick back and enjoy it, June," he said.

"I tried that," I protested. "But don't you honestly think it's a bit disgusting, if not mildly amusing, when the guy is on top and he moves up and that weird suction-farting noise screams across the room? PPPPTTTTT!!!" (#101)

Many people laughed, not only at the cool sound effects, but because they knew I was right. Some bizarre stuff happens during sex, and we all willingly ignore it in the name of passion. For years, I couldn't keep myself from laughing as I had sex with many guys, "researching" (as I called it) for more material for this book. It was fun while it lasted, but maybe, when it all comes down to it, I just wasn't kicking back and enjoying it. I couldn't enjoy it, because I was so busy pointing out the oddities of sex.

I probably would never have come up with this book if my first few sexual experiences were fun.

A Few Things I Hate about Sex

1. Don't ever use hot fudge or caramel sauce.

2. Sex on the beach is very romantic until sand gets in the way.

3. When my legs and butt are sore from having so much sex for the next two days.

4. When I can *feel* that whopper orgasm ready to hit, but it never comes.

5. I'm a TV freak, especially if we put in a movie that I like, so I really hate having sex when the tube is on.

6. When I let a guy eat me out, he's really fabulous, he knows what he's doing, he's great, and suddenly, I have real bad gas!!!

7. When a man doesn't understand the word, "OW!!"

8. When a guy rubs my clitoris so much it's really painful. The only reason why I'm twitching is because you hit a nerve. I'm really not enjoying this.

9. When a guy literally chews on my neck and he thinks I enjoy it. The only reason why I'm squirming is because it hurts, fucker.

10. When the sex is so bad, I have to stop and kick him out. "Look, dude, you're terrible. Please leave."

11. When I'm so tired and bored I have to stop the sex.

12. When I don't want to have sex with some guy and I have to imagine he's someone else.

13. When we're having sex in the car to loud music and wonderful heat, and we have to stop because the battery is dying.

14. When my tape player eats my favorite tape in the middle of sex.

15. When the CD starts skipping and we lose our rhythm.

16. The feminine fart. Yikes.

17. When my necklaces get in the way and slap him in the face while I'm riding him.

18. When my necklaces slam me in the face.

19. When he's riding me and my necklaces wrap around my neck and almost strangle me. Maybe I should just stop wearing long chained necklaces.

20. When he was drinking all day, and he convinces me to "make love," so I consent and not five minutes into the act, he goes limp because he was drinking so much.

21. When a guy does something to my inner thigh (a bite, a lick, whatever) and I can't really enjoy the intensity of it because I'm too busy concentrating on keeping my leg from twitching and slamming him in the face.

22. Right before we both cum, either I get a leg cramp or I get too tired.

23. Rug burn on my spine, dammit!! (Or rug burn anywhere, for that matter.)

24. When a guy gives me whisker burn *down there*.

25. When I have a yeast infection and I'm too embarrassed to tell him why we can't have sex, which makes him wonder why I've suddenly become a frigid bitch.

26. Check this out: A guy eats me out one night and I actually enjoyed it. Then he asks me the dumbest question I've ever heard: "Do you like how you taste?"

27. When a guy fingers me and shoves his finger in my mouth.

28. When I'm flirting with a guy and he somehow gets the idea that I'm an acrobat and I have trapezes and trampolines at my house.

29. When a guy is so small, there isn't a condom made that will fit him.

30. When the guy looses the condom inside me, *lies* about finding it on the floor and throwing it away, and then I find out two days later where it went when my body forces it out. Boy was I pissed!!

31. When the headboard on my bed slams up against the wall and my parents are downstairs.

32. When the stuff on my headboard falls and hits us in the head.

33. When a guy wants to use as many sex toys, food items, and/or bondage methods as possible in record time.

34. When a guy hushes me during sex.

35. When a guy grabs my hair and yanks my head back in the middle of a slow, easygoing lovemaking. That was totally unexpected.

36. When during foreplay, the guy hisses at me. Dork.

37. Sex in the shower. I'm always so scared to death that I'm going to slip and crack my head open, or the water goes up my nose during a certain position, or the water turns ice cold while we're going at it.

38. When someone farts during oral sex.

39. When I'm really tired, but he isn't, and he's getting hot and heavy and fooling around, then I fall asleep and he gets upset.

40. When we're done having sex and he wants me to take the condom off with my teeth.

41. Having sex stoned with a strobe light on. It makes me sick.

42. When the guy drools down my neck.

43. When I accidentally leave my underwear in his car.

44. When I do the aforementioned (#43) and he thinks it's a calling card.

45. When we're screwing in the driver's seat and one of us hits the horn.

46. When we're screwing in vinyl seats and the seat gets so wet, we slip everywhere.

47. Having sex in a Camaro.

48. When I have sex in a standard car, and I hit the gearshift, and since the emergency break doesn't work, we start rolling.

49. When we're getting all hot-n'-heavy in a car and the clutch is in the way, as well as the emergency break, the arm rest, the bump between the seats...

50. When I'm riding a guy in a car and my head keeps hitting the ceiling.

51. The unexpected period.

52. When a guy has a beard, he eats me out and I can smell my spooge in his beard two hours later.

53. When a guy's spooge is so bitter, it makes me heave.

54. When a guy boasts about his penis size and he's actually the size of a cocktail weenie, fully extended.

55. When my hair gets in my face.

56. When the guy wants me to put on the condom.

57. The 69 Position. I always get so into what he's doing for me, that I forget that I'm supposed to be doing something for him. I just can't multi-task like that.

58. When the deodorant suddenly fails.

59. When we're done screwing and the spooge from both of us oozes down my leg.

60. When a guy is eating me out, he comes up for a breath, and just when I think he's done, he continues.

61. When a guy expects me to blow him after we're finished.

62. When a guy fiercely bites my snatch.

63. When a guy eats me out and the slurping noises are so loud, I can't enjoy a damn thing.

64. Being throat fucked. I mean, I'm blowing him and he grabs my head and shoves himself down my throat so deep, I gag.

65. Having sex on a hardwood floor that hasn't been refinished in decades and we both get splinters in bizarre places where we're not supposed to get splinters.

66. Having sex on a linoleum floor and getting floor burn, totally different from rug burn.

67. When the guy thrusts so deep into me, it feels like my entrails have been seriously compacted and are ready to come out of my mouth.

68. When a guy has hangnails so bad that when he fingers me, it feels like he's scraping me out with a fork.

69. When a guy tells me to scream, then hushes me when I do.

70. When we're done screwing and I roll over onto a wet spot.

71. When a guy wants to screw me while I'm on the rag. I'm sorry, that's too messy.

72. When a guy gives me sexual looks and it looks like he has no clue what he's doing, but he's actually serious.

73. When a guy gives me sexual looks and it looks like he knows what he's doing so he gets me excited, then I find out that he's actually totally clueless.

74. When I'm riding a guy and he gets so excited that he decides to take over and he slips out.

75. When a guy is too small and he constantly slips out.

76. When a guy is so horny, he has to have sex every day, five times a day.

77. When I have sex with a guy and he lays a guilt trip on me afterwards. What the hell is that all about?

78. When a guy goes to grab my breasts and says, "Hey, where'd they go?"

79. When a guy pinches and nibbles my nipples too hard.

80. When a guy wants me to have sex with another woman so he can watch. I'll do that after he has sex with another man so *I* can watch.

81. When a guy wants me to masturbate for him without my vibrator and I'm not in the mood.

82. When a guy decides to surprise me with one huge painful thrust after a series of soft, gentle, enjoyable thrusts.

83. When I blow a guy, he dies in ecstasy, and right before he spooges, he grabs my hair and yanks my head back, and I get a load in the eye. (Ooooww-www!! It burns!! It burns!!!!)

84. When a guy wants to doggie-do me, and he gets the wrong hole. Ouch.

85. When a guy wants to try sodomy without my permission, sans the lube.

86. When I get pubes caught between my teeth.

87. When I cough up pubes.

88. When I get pubes caught in the back of my throat and I didn't even blow him.

89. When the guy wants to screw me in eight different positions in record time.

90. When we're screwing in a small space and my head hits something metal.

91. When a guy asks me if I'm enjoying myself.

92. When a guy gets too "into" one part of my snatch.

93. When I give a guy sexual hints and he doesn't pick up on them.

94. When a guy wants me to blow him, so he ever-so-subtly shoves my head in his crotch.

95. When I go to the bathroom after sex and it burns.

96. When a guy wants to screw me doggie-style, so he gets me on my knees, puts my feet up to my butt, and forcefully spreads my legs apart.

97. When we're screwing missionary, I go to claw at his back and I end up ripping open a few zits.

98. The squishing noises.

99. Not being able to bite and claw.

100. When a guy moves up and the friction from the sweat of our bodies causes a weird suction farting noise.

101. When a guy puts on a condom in front of me and gives me sexual looks. I'm sorry, I just find that funny.

102. When, after sex, a guy is cocky enough to say, "Was I not great or what?"

103. When a guy squirts in two minutes, rolls over, and falls asleep. Meanwhile, I'm horny as hell.

104. When a guy wants to keep going when I'm bone dry.

105. When I can't walk afterwards.

106. When a guy wants to have just sex—no foreplay.

107. When a guy tells me I'm "So Beautiful" in the eye of passion.

108. When I can hear everything that goes on during sex.

109. When I'm hungry during sex and my stomach growls.

110. When we somehow head-butt in the middle of a passionate frenzy.

111. When the massage lotions are cold.

112. Giving handjobs with no lubrication.

113. When I go to peck a guy on the mouth and he thinks it's a major French kiss and I pull away with slobber all over my face.

114. When a guy can't control his saliva glands and I end up with drool all over my body.

115. When in the middle of a passionate frenzy, the guy shoves his finger up my butt. "WHOA!!! Steady there, killer!!! Exit only!!!"

116. When a guy is screwing me doggie-style, it lasts for half and hour, he finishes and rolls over and falls asleep. Meanwhile, I'm frozen in the doggie-style position.

117. When a guy jacks off and begs me to lick it off his stomach.

118. When a guy wants to be inventive and says, "HEY!!! Let's try the wheelbarrow position!"

119. When a guy goes down on me and looks up every so often to see if I'm enjoying myself.

120. When a guy expects me to suck on his finger during foreplay. I'll suck on something, just not your finger. I don't see the romance in it.

121. When, in the middle of screwing, a fart escapes one of our bodies.

122. When a guy is so big he rips me in half.

123. Stoned sex.

124. Drunk sex.

125. When I don't realize that I'm giving him sexual looks and he's all over me, and I'm totally clueless as to what's going on. Then he gets upset.

126. "Baby, I'm like the Energizer Rabbit. I can keep going, and going, and going..." (i.e., when a guy says anything he can to get into bed with me.)

127. When a man doesn't cum. When he's so interested in getting me to cum that he doesn't think about himself. It's one thing to want me to cum, but to make a complete mission out of it while sacrificing your own pleasure isn't pleasurable or romantic to me.

128. When a guy talks to me during sex. Dude, shut up. I'm trying to enjoy myself.

129. When a guy has to ask questions while we're screwing. "Ooh, do you like that? How's that, baby? Yeah, that's it…*grunt* Yeah, right there. Ungh. Are you likin' that, baby? Oh, yeah…"

130. When I see a kickass position on a porn site and I can't emulate it to save my life.

A Few Things
I Love about Sex

Well, I kicked back and enjoyed it. Figure that one out, eh? I don't really hate sex anymore, but this list is also comprised of things that we women want to have men do during sex, as well as what we like about it. But since men don't usually know what to do, I figured I'd write this so that they could get a clue. Don't worry, a lot of women have read this and agree wholeheartedly with me on what men should and shouldn't do during sex. So guys, read closely and take notes. We women expect to see some improvements.

A Few Things I Love about Sex

1. When a guy doesn't push my head into his crotch when I go to blow him.

2. Hearing those cute little sighs escape his lips.

3. When he spooges on my back.

4. The doggie-style position.

5. When he hugs me during sex.

6. When everything goes smoothly.

7. When he ignores the few select sounds that may escape my body in the heat of passion.

8. Riding a guy.

9. Being fingered while the guy is inside me.

10. Turning a guy on.

11. Biting.

12. Scratching.

13. When he gently runs his fingernails all over my body.

14. When he runs his hands through my hair and brings my smiling face to his for a passionate kiss.

15. Kissing.

16. Kissing a guy all over his face and body.

17. Using my tongue to turn a guy on.

18. Giving backrubs with warm massage oils.

19. When I nibble on a guy's ear and he moans and giggles.

20. When I give a guy a nut-rub and he goes nuts (no pun intended).

21. When a guy gives me a light body rub after sex.

22. When a guy sniffs my neck and chuckles like a dirty old man.

23. When a man cums inside me.

24. When he sucks in a breath and shudders in ecstasy when he cums. I know I did something right.

25. Lighting up a cigarette for him after sex.

26. When he goes down on me, he knows what he's doing and it actually feels good!!!

27. When a guy has a beard and he goes down on me and it tickles.

28. When a guy tickles me and it turns me on.

29. When a guy hoists me over his shoulder and carries me into the bedroom.

30. When he hops on top of me.

31. Orgasms.

32. When we have sex at night and he wakes up in the morning feeling like a million bucks.

33. When a guy makes me feel so good, I want to scream.

34. When a guy is so proud that he got an "Oh, GOD!!" or an "Oh, SHIT!!" out of me, he tells everyone.

35. When a guy thrusts into me doggie-style and I just feel this wave of fanatical ecstasy pulse through my body.

36. When he's open about our sexual experiences with each other, and lets me know what he likes, how it feels for him, and what he'd like to try.

37. When the sexual hints he gives me are cute.

38. Having sex on the floor.

39. Having sex on the bed.

40. When after sex, I can roll over and put my arm around him and he'll press up against me with a satisfied moan.

41. When he's screwing me doggie-style and I can feel his testicles bump into me.

42. When he's doggie-doing me and he leans down to kiss my neck or nibble on my ear.

43. When I see a smile on his face as I'm riding him.

44. When we're in the missionary position and he hugs me closely and breathes heavily in my ear.

45. When after sex, I'm lying there awake and he rolls over and puts his arm around me.

46. When I'm riding him and I look down to see him gazing at me through half-open eyes.

47. When he pants heavily in my ear.

48. When I get an "Oh, YES!!" out of him.

49. When we have sex in the shower and I don't slip.

50. When I'm just standing there and my boyfriend just comes up behind me and hugs me closely.

51. When we have sex in a dimly lit room with loud music.

52. When we're so close, I can feel his heartbeat.

53. Lying on top of him.

54. Orgasms.

55. When he lies on top of me.

56. Necking sessions every now and again.

57. Sex with feeling. Oooohhh, sex with feeling.

58. Sex to hard, heavy music that arouses the mind as well as the body.

59. When we're someplace public and he turns to me and says something like, "What say we have sex on that thing right there?" or "How 'bout if I just bend you over on this table right here and screw your brains out?"

60. When a guy kisses, nibbles, and sucks on my neck without leaving hickies.

61. When a guy can give me goose bumps all over my body.

62. When a guy runs his fingers lightly over my skin.

63. When a guy is hard as a rock throughout the whole session of sex.

64. When the sex is so intense, we roll all over the bed, the floor, the hallway, the kitchen…

65. When our bodies rub together during intercourse.

66. When I "tease" him so much, he goes nuts and basically attacks me.

67. When we accidentally slam our heads and it'll either go unnoticed or we can laugh about it.

68. When I give a successful handjob.

69. When I give a great blowjob and he's so happy that I swallowed.

70. When he doesn't force me to swallow his spooge.

71. When I get lost in his eyes.

72. Having sex on a soft chair where I straddle and ride him like the wind.

73. When after sex, I notice him staring at me lovingly out of the corner of my eye.

74. When the sex is so good, I want to run around in the street, hooting and hollering at the top of my lungs, laughing and high-fiving trees and signs.

75. When the sex is so good, I can't wipe the ecstatic grin off my face for days.

76. When we're screwing and I still can't get over how beautifully sculpted his body is.

77. When he lights up a cigarette for me after sex.

78. When I'm so excited that all I want to do is throw him around, chain him up, and screw him into a coma.

79. When he gives me a hickey on my lips. I can almost feel the kiss for days afterward.

80. Orgasms!!!!!

81. Sex when it's slow, deep, and hard.

82. When the guy I'm totally in love with is just inside me, no pushing, no thrusting, nothing but filling me up.

83. When we both just talk to each other after the deed about what we liked and what we want to try the next time.

84. When we're just lying there naked after sex and our legs are intertwined.

85. When he's rough-n'-tough and ready to rumble.

86. Astronomical sex.

87. The fantastic sex that physically lasts five to ten minutes, but mentally lasts for two days.

88. Foreplay.

89. When he undresses me.

90. To giggle during foreplay.

91. Spontaneous sex, the kind where neither one of us has planned it, then all of a sudden, the next thing we know, we're all over each other in a passionate frenzy.

92. To tickle a guy into a wrestling match that guarantees a good night of passionate, unadulterated sex.

93. When after sex, we just lay there and talk about everything under the sun and moon.

94. When I pin his arms immobile and he likes it.

95. When I'm having sex with the guy I love and he shows me he loves me through passionate lovemaking.

96. When we cum together.

97. When we kiss so passionately, I feel like we're gonna eat each other up while we're having sex.

98. The after-sex rubdown.

99. Giving him backrubs while he's cumming.

100. Turning him on with body rubs.

101. Taking baths by candlelight with him.

102. When there's romance, dreamlike romance.

103. When he continuously makes me cum and he hasn't even started yet.

104. Did I say orgasms?

105. That pulsing white light that starts in my hips and floods through my body, making every nerve tingle through to the tips of my toes and fingers, then finally warming my face, making my skin ripple and my body twitch.

106. When he can make me cum with his fingers.

107. When he enjoys making me feel like a really sexy woman, not a love toy.

108. When we screw the brains out of each other and end up in a gasping heap on the bed.

109. When he understands and still loves me and still wants to have sex with me after I tell him that I have Genital Herpes.

110. When I have nothing on my mind but him, pleasing him, and how much I love him.

111. When he ties me up and blindfolds me so all I can do is feel.

112. The initial penetration.

113. Girth over length, but length still rocks.

114. When his naked chest is pressed up against mine.

115. Nuzzling.

116. When he thinks of me during sex.

117. When I think of him.

118. That cute little patch of hair between his pecs.

119. Kissable lips.

120. Agile fingers.

121. Great hands.

122. Strong shoulders.

123. Endurance and stamina.

124. When he does everything in his power to make sure I've cum a billion times before he lets loose and cums.

125. Sex on the day after I finish my period.

126. Sex in the wintertime when it's snowing outside and we're all nice and warm and a fire is lit.

127. Mutual masturbation.

128. Playing with myself in front of him.

129. Sex right after I get out of the shower.

130. Sex with no worries about anything.

131. When the sex is still exciting after being with him for so long.

132. When we have sex after a week or two of waiting.

A Few Things
We Women Hate about Men

I love men, I really do. They're such sweethearts when they want to be. But man, oh, man, can they just pick at that little nerve of intolerance that we women have! I'm not just talking about the little things like leaving whiskers on the sink, and not putting the toilet seat down (as frustrating as those are sometimes). No, I'm talking about their insane ability to laugh at me when I'm emotional, or when they *have* to tickle me when I have to pee. So, all the guys reading this, I can just hear you gloating. "Yah, I do that. Hahaha." Yeah, dude, gloat. Laugh your little butt off. Just you wait.

A Few Things Women Hate about Men

1. When guys leave the toilet seat up.

2. When guys leave whiskers all over the sink.

3. When guys have really nice butts, but they wear baggy pants.

4. When a guy answers questions with "because."

5. When I'm talking to a guy on the phone and I have to keep repeating myself because he's paying more attention to the TV than to me.

6. When a guy says he's not a breast man, but I see him drooling over Miss July's boobs in *Playboy*.

7. When a guy won't introduce me to his parents because I'm "too weird," yet he's the one who owns the handcuffs, the skulls, and the whips.

8. When a guy won't father his children but insists on winning a pool tournament.

9. When a guy constantly wants me to page him, but he never calls back.

10. When I spend all of my hard earned money helping him live, and he won't even kiss me on Valentine's Day, let alone get me a card.

11. When a guy tells me he loves me but all he wants is sex.

12. When a guy won't understand the crisis I'm going through.

13. When a guy soups up his car, but won't spend any money on me.

14. When my guy forgets our anniversary.

15. When my guy wants me to come pick him up and when I get to his house, he's still in his boxers writing a *Dungeons & Dragons* adventure.

16. Obsessive men.

17. When a guy gets mad at me for doing something to my hair, but he won't even wash his.

18. When a guy cheats on me.

19. Male Chauvinist Pigs.

20. Ignorant men.

21. When a man thinks he's God's gift to women.

22. When a guy tells me I need to conquer my past when his own life is in a shambles because he can't conquer his own demons.

23. When a guy constantly scratches his crotch in public.

24. When nice guys die.

25. When a guy seems so unapproachable, all I can do is stare.

26. When a guy is too hard to talk to.

27. When guys play clueless.

28. When a guy stares at me and doesn't have the guts to come over and talk to me.

29. When a guy stares at my chest when I talk.

30. When guys get stupid tattoos like Tasmanian Devils and sports logos on their bodies and they think they're cool.

31. When my boyfriend isn't in my immediate environment and I get so lonely without him.

32. When I can't tell if a guy is male of female.

33. When a guy mistakes me for a fellow brother.

34. When guys drool over Japanese animation chicks or other cartoon characters.

35. When a guy says, "Would you mind staying home with the kids while I go out with the guys?" and they're not even my kids.

36. When a guy picks out our children's names when I didn't even know we were going out.

37. Male mood swings.

38. When a guy feels the need to belittle me in public.

39. When I bitch a guy out and he always responds with, "Yeah, whatever."

40. Clingy guys.

41. When I have a crush on a guy and he claims he has no luck with women.

42. When a guy expresses his love for me through rapping. I hate rap.

43. When a guy finds out that I have a crush on him and he makes me feel stupid for ever wanting to have anything with him.

44. When a guy thinks his looks are his main staple in life.

45. When a guy sits there and promises me roses and doesn't do anything about it.

46. When one guy apologizes for raping me by giving me flowers.

47. When a guy screws some girl behind my back and his excuse is "I was sick of jacking off."

48. When a man pretends to know what I'm talking about.

49. When he tells me I'm his life right within the first week of dating.

50. When a guy doesn't know how to act around me and I can tell.

51. When a guy stares at me lustfully with his girlfriend on his arm.

52. When my sister's boyfriend tells me I'm the coolest chick he's ever known.

53. When a guy thinks he's too good for me.

54. Alcoholic men.

55. When a guy doesn't tell me the truth because he thinks I can't handle it.

56. When men spit.

57. When men aren't sympathetic when I have cramps or PMS.

58. When I have a problem that isn't destined to go away anytime soon and he won't talk about it, let alone acknowledge it.

59. When a guy thinks it's funny to tickle me when I have to pee. I'm serious: This is no laughing matter.

60. When a guy teases me all in the name of fun, but the teasing is completely mean and destructive.

61. When a guy knows I like him, so he ignores me.

62. When a guy waits for me to start a conversation.

63. When a guy waits for me to approach him.

64. When guys won't tell me the truth until it's too late.

65. When guys laugh or scoff at me when I cry.

66. When men are "always right."

67. When a guy has to fight to prove himself.

68. When I break up with a guy and he stalks me.

69. When my guy friend wants me to stalk his ex-girlfriend with him.

70. When a guy's idea of being romantic is buying the condom.

71. When guys expect me to constantly give them backrubs.

72. When guys talk in a baby voice.

73. When guys overdose on cologne.

74. When a guy is over-possessive.

75. When a guy says I don't love him just because I won't have sex with him right off the bat.

76. When a guy says he hates gossip, but wastes no time telling the world about me.

77. When a guy expects me to eat every time he does.

78. When guys know how to piss me off.

79. When men insist I would "never understand" their plights, problems, or demons.

80. When men won't listen to anything I have to say.

81. When a guy is intimidated by gay men because gay men get along better with women.

82. When a guy won't leave me alone when I need time to myself.

83. When a guy makes jokes about me and my idiosyncrasies after sex.

84. The "Wham, Bam, Thank You, Ma'am!" guys.

85. The following combination: men and videogames.

86. When I'm too normal for Punk Rock guys, too Punk Rock for normal guys, and there's no in-between.

87. When guys tell me it's unattractive for women to smoke, yet every time I see a guy at a stoplight, I see him picking his nose.

88. When I go out of my way to make a prospective boyfriend happy, and I see another woman on his arm without a word of warning.

89. When I see my sister's boyfriend with another woman and he begs me not to tell her.

90. When I snore in front of a guy and he makes fun of me for it.

91. When a guy is talking to me incessantly while I'm falling asleep, and he won't stop gabbing away.

92. When a guy stares at me and starts to drool. I actually had that happen.

93. Any man under the age of sixty who can't control his salivary glands.

94. When seventeen-year-old guys are complete assholes to me because I don't fit their bill of the perfect woman. Wait until you're older, sport.

95. When a guy tells me I "disobeyed" him.

96. Hypocritical men.

97. When a guy won't let me wear certain clothes because other people will see what I "look like."

A Few Things
We Women Love about Men

No matter how many times I've come home complaining about the many things gone wrong in my life, my boyfriend always has the time to listen. When I went crazy, he stuck by me. He went (willingly) to many Christmas dinners with my family; he supported me when I changed careers and went back to school. He's been there all the way. This list is dedicated to him.

I love you, Cliff.

A Few Things Women Love about Men

1. When a guy curls up behind me after sex and wraps me up in his strong arms.

2. When a guy stops what he's doing, comes over to me, and kisses me softly on the lips.

3. The way my man smells.

4. When a guy grabs my hips and kisses me relentlessly.

5. When a guy invites me over to his house to have dinner with his family.

6. When a guy lets me initiate sex.

7. When two guys hug in friendship.

8. When a guy comes up to me and asks for a hug.

9. Watching a group of guys sitting around having a good time.

10. When a guy will listen to what I have to say.

11. When a guy will just look at me and smile.

12. When a guy tells me that everything is going to be okay and he means it.

13. When a guy lights my cigarette.

14. When he realizes that I'm cold, so he opens up his jacket and holds me inside.

15. When he laces up my boots for me.

16. When he just looks at me and says, "You know, I think you're cool."

17. When he massages my head.

18. When a guy can come to me and trust me enough with his problems.

19. When a guy lets me sit in his chair.

20. Optimistic men.

21. When I do something stupid and the guy will laugh at the thing I did instead of at me.

22. When he takes only three minutes to pack his things for a trip.

23. When he trusts me enough to cut his hair.

24. When he lets me use his bathrobe when I take a shower at his house.

25. Watching guys shave.

26. When he shaves my legs.

27. When he lets me vent on him, and doesn't take it personally.

28. When I wake up and realize my guy was watching me in my sleep.

29. When I fall asleep on the floor and my guy will put a blanket over me and lay next to me instead of going to bed.

30. When he lets me play D.J. on his car stereo.

31. When my guy brushes the hair out of my eyes.

32. When my guy knows when I just want to lay in bed and not have sex.

33. When he puts a nice, fresh warm towel around me when I get out of the bathtub or shower.

34. When he knows when to shut up.

35. When a guy will look me straight in the face and tell me the truth, no matter how bad it hurts.

36. When I don't want to have sex and he doesn't take it personally.

37. When I buy a vibrator or other fem-toys and he doesn't take it personally.

38. When he knows I don't want to have sex, and I don't have to tell him.

39. Guys who are their own person.

40. A guy who can admit his own feelings.

41. Guys with a great sense of humor.

42. When he lets me wear his clothes.

43. When he buys a sweater for himself and tells me that I would look good in it if I wanted to wear it.

44. When a guy tells me stories with such enthusiasm, I get completely engrossed in not only the story, but him and his storytelling abilities.

45. When a guy wants to sit at home and watch movies.

46. When my guy comes up behind me and puts his arms around me.

47. When he gets excited because I helped him solve a problem he's been working on for a while. For instance, my boyfriend is writing a children's book. It's small, consisting of little stories. Well, he couldn't—for the life of him—figure out how to end one of the stories. After I read it and gave him my own view of the ending, he was able to integrate our ideas together, and now it's one of our favorite stories to share with people. I'm so proud.

48. When he respects my opinions and asks for guidance when he feels he needs it.

49. When he smiles at me for no reason.

50. When he reaches over and touches my arm, my hand, or my shoulder in front of my family.

51. When we go into a store and he grabs my hand and holds it.

52. That little kid inside of him that keeps him young and vibrant.

53. When he sees a vase or a picture frame I might like, so he gets excited to show me and leads me through the store like a little kid who just found his perfect toy.

54. When he remembers me when he goes out to get some groceries and gets me some of my favorite candies, or tampons, or a bouquet of flowers.

55. When a guy stares at me and when I ask him why, he says, "Because I like looking at you."

56. When a guy drives with a cigarette hanging out of his mouth.

57. When he tells me I'm beautiful with or without the make-up and means it.

58. When I sleep with him and he shares his pillow (not to mention the blankets) with me.

59. Watching my man sleep.

60. When a guy feels totally comfortable around me.

61. When he doesn't forget to introduce me to his family, friends, coworkers, boss, etc.

62. When he is willing to meet with my parents.

63. When he can hold better conversations with my family than I can.

64. When he's willing to sit there and listen to my family's depressing stories.

65. When he's so proud of me and my heritage.

66. When he totally respects the fact that all I need to do is get blasted every once in a while.

67. When he sticks up for me when somebody puts me down.

68. When he misses me.

69. When he tells me he loves me.

70. When he can laugh at himself.

71. Broad muscular shoulders. Yum.

72. When he hugs me because he wants to, not because he feels he has to.

73. When he does things for me that I'd never expect him to do: buys me flowers, takes me out to a nice restaurant, dedicates a meaningful song to me, etc.

74. When he doesn't complain about what I might do with my hair that week.

75. When he surprises me by suddenly getting intimate with me in public.

76. When he looks at me and winks.

77. When a guy knows the difference between a friendship and a relationship.

78. When a guy takes off his shirt and his body is so beautiful that I have to literally smack myself in the face.

79. When a guy—boyfriend or friend—doesn't try to run my life.

80. When my guy is a lot like my dad ('cuz dad was the coolest guy in the world!!), but he is also his own entity.

81. When he drinks, knows when to quit, and respects me if I don't want to do it.

82. When he acknowledges my presence after being in the same room with me for several hours.

83. Rubbing my man's tummy and thighs.

84. Seeing guys giggle.

85. When a guy admits that he just wants to be held and talked to, and that sex would be good, but it's not necessary.

86. When a guy makes me blush.

87. When I can make him blush.

88. When my man understands my problems and helps me deal with them.

89. When my man is patient with me.

90. When my man lets me pick out his outfit every once in a while.

91. When he knows I'm depressed and does my household chores for me.

92. When my man has achievable goals, does everything in his power to reach those goals, and doesn't forget me in the meantime.

93. When he stops by my work because he missed me.

94. When he teases me and makes it clear that it's all in the name of fun. Hey, I can laugh at myself every now and again.

95. When I tease him and he knows I'm only joking.

96. When he laughs at my quips, jokes, one-liners, etc.

97. When he understands my complaining, but is able to be honest with me about the validity of my gripes.

98. When he runs his hands all over my body like I'm made of the most precious stones in the world.

99. When he'll wrestle with me.

100. When he can relate to my problems.

101. When he has the ability to empathize with me.

102. When, even though he's not in a great mood, he still lets me hug him and care for him.

103. When he worries about me.

104. When we agree to disagree and we respect each other's opinions.

105. When he's open to suggestions and constructive criticism.

106. When he can take criticism gracefully.

107. When he loves me for who I am.

A Few Things
Women Hate about Each Other

Through the years, I have come to the conclusion that certain women on this planet are either completely stupid or just don't think. Who knows, I might be one of them. I do know, however, that one way of discovering more about yourself is to see yourself in other people. It's funny, too, the stuff you come up with. In writing this list, back in '98, I was just ranting. I hate this, and I hate that, and some women piss me off to no end!! As I looked back on it today, I noticed that half of the list contains stuff that I do or did on a regular basis. Take, for instance, that one chick who *has* to put on make-up at a stoplight. Done it. Or that girl who gossips about the stupidest stuff. Yep, that's me. Or that one chick who sprays the perfume on so heavily, you gag. I've done that, too. Maybe just once, but I've done it. And in realizing that I am the culprit of such trivial stuff, I got worried. What's the stuff that I've never done? What kind of little idiosyncrasies do I have that other people hate about me? Well, I came up with a few, and in doing so, I came up with more mature points about what women just can't stand about each other. And working with 90 percent women helps out a lot. Just one day at my job fills in over half of this list. So, to my fellow sisters out there, I really hope you get a good laugh out of this. After all, we are women, and we are only human, right?

A Few Things We Women Hate about Each Other

1. Women's innate ability to be so catty, it's almost comical.

2. When a woman thinks I'm staring lustfully at her man, when I'm really just zoning out.

3. When women complain about everything being unsanitary, yet they leave their dirty tampons on the bathroom floor.

4. Women who think they're awesome and rub it in my face that they're "better than" me.

5. When lesbians hit on me incessantly. It's flattering at first, but honestly, when you see me getting uncomfortable, stop.

6. The Perfect Women. Meaning those girls that you never see fart or have a zit, who have perfect hair, nails, and lipstick, not to mention beautiful teeth, fantastic bodies, and a wonderful personality to boot. These women are born with it, and it's definitely not Maybelline.

7. When I go into the bathroom after some "perfect" girl and the john reeks of CK ONE and hairspray.

8. When women bitch, moan, and complain about not having a man, then I see them hitting on my boyfriend.

9. When women think that a tattoo or piercing makes them more alluring/tough/mysterious. (Note: sometimes they're right in that thinking.)

10. Girls who like to pick fights with *anyone.*

11. Those chicks who make me feel their pregnant bellies.

12. Girls who put on nail polish in public. The stench just kills me.

13. Girls who give me dirty looks from across a room, but don't have the courage to pick a fight with me. Must be my tattoos that intimidate them.

14. Girls who pick fights knowing that their boyfriends will back them up.

15. Those chicks who have roses and hearts tattooed on their inner hips or ankles.

16. Large women in spandex.

17. When chicks get dressed up to go to the mall/gas station/bank/oil change service.

18. Girls who wear white tank tops with no brassieres out in public.

19. When chicks are really bitchy and mean to me, then try to bum cigarettes off of me.

20. When a girl changes her entire lifestyle for a guy.

21. When some girl thinks I'm pretty cool, then I end up with a twin.

22. Women who wear Daisy Duke Short Shorts and their lumpy butts hang out.

23. When I know a girl doesn't like me, but she's all peaches-n'-cream to my face.

24. When I confide in a chick about something, she promises not to tell a soul, then the next day, it's all over town.

25. Women who rub it in my face that they have boyfriends.

26. Preachy women.

27. When women smack around their really cool boyfriends.

28. When one of my guy friends' girlfriends comes to me to bitch about him.

29. When girls think I'm a butch lesbian just because I shaved my head.

30. Skinchicks who want to beat me up just because I have a shaved head and they think that I'm some part of a rival band of skinheads. I'm not even a skinhead!!

31. When a woman mistakes me for a guy just because of my shaved head.

32. Women who use abortion as a method of birth control.

33. Women who smoke the following:
Any Ultra Light 120
Any Ultra Light Menthol 120
Any cigarette where the nicotine level is practically nonexistent.
Then these chicks claim to go through nicotine withdrawal. I'm sorry, but I smoke non-filtered cigarettes, and let me tell you, you haven't experienced what I've experienced. These nicotine fits are class-A, number one lethal.

34. Teeny-bopper chicks who think it's cool to smoke, so I watch them go through a whole pack of cigarettes without smoking more than half of the cigarette and without inhaling. If you're gonna smoke, smoke. Don't act like it. It's a waste.

35. Those little girls who giggle too loudly and flirt outrageously with every guy they see.

36. Hearing about 13-year-olds who are pregnant with their second child. Where are these kids' parents?

37. Watching talk shows where the 13-year-old is pregnant with her second child and her mother—who had already had four kids by the age of 15—can't understand what went wrong.

38. When women with big breasts rub it in my face that guys like them better because they're well-endowed.

39. Women with no morals or values.

40. Over-dramatic women.

41. Women who can't handle the truth.

42. Girls who walk around thinking they're God's gift to men.

43. Those chicks who have to say "EEEWW!!" to everything. I actually heard this once, I swear on my father's grave: "Oh, my GAWD!! You've never seen that movie? Eeeww! How gross!!" Verbatim. Now, tell me, how is it gross that someone has never seen a specific movie? I just don't get it. Eeeww.

44. The fact that all women, myself included, are back-stabbing, selfish bitches.

45. When some chick I don't know tells me what my boyfriend is doing behind my back with her. "Just so you know. I felt guilty."

46. When chicks ask me to check their butts for bloodstains. Gross, no?

47. When some chicks have to one-up me in the man department.

48. When some God-awful ugly chick rubs it in my face that she's seeing my ex-boyfriend.

49. When some chick rubs it in my face that she's dating the guy I have a crush on.

50. Those little groups of 14-year-olds that get really silent and start to giggle as I walk by.

51. Those chicks who have to have a man no matter what the cost, and it's usually my man.

52. Those chicks who "need" a man to do all the dirty work, then bitch about not being allowed to do anything.

53. Those chicks who take anti-depressants for attention.

54. Those women who spoil their kids, then wonder why their children are so selfish and mean.

55. Women who breastfeed in public.

56. Those women who set their grubby, dirty little kids on the counters of fast food joints. Hey, my food is going on that counter, do you mind!!??

57. Women who let their little monsters drool, bite, and grab everything in sight in public. "No, Bobby, don't do that. Bobby, come here. Bobby, I'm gonna spank your butt, now come here. Bobby, come here. Here. HERE!!! BOBBY!!!"

58. Those chicks who think they're fat and make their weight a public issue, when they're thinner than me.

59. I hate women who gossip, but did you hear about that girl who…?

60. Getting stuck at a stoplight behind that one girl who *has* to put on her make-up, do her hair, shave her legs, and talk on her cell phone.

61. Women who wear ankle bracelets *underneath* their nylons.

62. Pompous women.

63. Those chicks that can eat everything in sight and not gain a pound.

64. Those chicks that walk around with their cell phones glued to their ears.

65. Those chicks who don't know how to drive an SUV.

66. Chicks that don't want to get fat, but they drink beer.

67. Those chicks who tell the most pointless stories I've ever heard: "My mom made pasta the other day." "Yeah, and…?" "And it was really good."

68. Those chicks who are insanely book smart, but get them behind the counter at McDonald's and they're totally clueless.

69. The women who make such a big deal out of nothing. "Oh, NO!!! My nail broke!!"

70. Those chicks who get so mad at the stupidest things. "Why did you put the napkins there? I told you not to put the napkins there; I wanted them over there!! Jeez, can't you do anything right?!"

71. Those girls who have to make my life a living hell because I'm not like them.

72. Obnoxious women.

73. Those chicks that always have to yell.

74. Those women who *have* to press every single little one of my buttons and test their boundaries with me and other people.

75. Women who are more talented than me, dammit.

76. Women who know exactly who they are and let you know about it to the point of being obnoxious.

77. I personally can't deal with those ladies who are neurotic clean freaks. "OH MY GOD, don't put that there!!! I just bleached that!!!!" "Well, where can I put it?" "I don't know!! Just don't put it there!!!"

78. Women who have a point of view and dammit, they will drill it clean into your head until you agree with them. This goes far beyond the whole "Preachy women" deal.

79. Manipulative women.

80. Deceitful women.

81. Women who lie about something, get caught in the lie, then keep it going like it's their last dying cause.

82. Women who lie about everything: who they talk to, what they do on a daily basis, who they sleep with, what they hate and like, etc.

83. Those ladies who have to repeat everything they say: "I need that decaf. Did I say decaf? Yeah, tell her that's decaf. Honey, that's decaf. Yeah, decaf." So...decaf, right?

84. Those women who just can't shut up. You know that one lady who has a story for everything, and man, she'll tell it to you whether you want to hear it or not.

85. Women who complain. Wait a minute...

Some Things
I Hate about Being a Woman

There are times when we women can't stand being female. Even though we're proud of who and what we are, there are days when even the slightest aspect of womanhood just aggravates us to no end. And so, during a rather trying day in my life, a long time ago, I wrote these moments down. And when I found this list after five years, I enjoyed it thoroughly. The sarcasm, the subtle humor, the points that we women think at least once in our lifetimes. So here it is, the trials and tribulations of being a woman, spilled out uncensored for the world to see.

This list is not for the squeamish.

Some Things I Hate about Being a Woman

1. The ability to jump to conclusions at the drop of a hat.

2. Menstruation.

3. My superior emotional roller coaster.

4. Cramps.

5. Bloating.

6. Why do guys like breasts so much?

7. Women's public restrooms. They can be so gross at times.

8. I'm honest with you once and suddenly I'm some sort of stark raving bitch.

9. I can't go a day without gossiping about something.

10. Just because a guy buys me dinner, I have to put out for him.

11. The paranoia.

12. Once a month, I get to shove a piece of cotton in a hole that wasn't meant for cotton, or I get to wear a diaper-like thing between my legs.

13. Body hair.

14. My ability to easily get breast, cervical, ovarian, and uterine cancer.

15. Other women!!!

16. Wearing make-up to be beautiful.

17. My uncanny ability to weep hysterically at the drop of a hat.

18. Because I'm a woman, it's gross for me to pick my nose, hock a loogie, and burp or fart in public.

19. Yeast infections.

20. Cysts in the damnedest places.

21. Binding undergarments.

22. When the pad shifts.

23. When the tampon leaks.

24. I have to put weird shit in my hair to make it look nice.

25. Thank God we don't have to wear corsets nowadays!!!

26. That strange odor that my body decides to give off at the most inopportune times.

27. I shave my legs in the winter, then get out of the shower, and the hair grows back immediately.

28. Ingrown hairs.

29. Waxing hurts.

30. Depilatory creams don't work.

31. Razors cut the dickens out of my skin.

32. Electrolysis costs too much.

33. Cramps!!!!

34. PMS.

35. DMS (During the Menstrual Syndrome).

36. Post-MS (Post Menstrual Syndrome).

37. Pregnancy mood swings.

38. My sister's hair was down to her butt in high school. Every morning, she had to deep condition and comb it for half an hour. Miraculously, nobody noticed or said a word to her about how beautiful and lustrous her hair was. Now that it's short (cropped above the ears), everyone tells her to grow it out.

39. I am a woman, therefore I am weak.

40. My shoulder blades stick out farther than my breasts ever will.

41. I have this insatiable addiction to chocolate.

42. Thanks to PMS, I get to be bloated, my chest hurts, and my mood swings are out the door.

43. I'm a woman, therefore, I love girlie stuff.

44. I'm a woman, so I have to smoke cigarettes like Virginia Slim Menthol Ultra Light 120's in a box.

45. If a guy doesn't call me when he says he'll call, I instantly think he's found another woman, and I somehow convince myself that he doesn't want to be with me because I'm ugly, incompetent, and insecure, and I get mad and depressed. It turns out that he didn't call because he chipped a tooth and had to go to the dentist.

46. Being the neutral person suddenly thrown in the middle of my two feuding best friends.

47. The stupidest things will annoy the hell out of me, like one stray hair out of place, accidentally smudging my eyeliner or lipstick, or getting my nail ripped off.

48. Maybelline and Cover Girl say my make-up will stay on for hours, then I discover smudged eyeliner, foundation stains, and lipstick, eye shadow, and mascara stains all over my shirts.

49. Gay men who look prettier than me, dammit!!

50. If my boyfriend is so pleased with the way I look, act, and treat him, then why is he checking out that hot blonde over there?

51. Fourteen-year-old girls who are more developed than me.

52. CRAMPS!!!!

53. Huh? What? I don't get it.

54. I am blonde, therefore I am a ding-dong.

55. Postpartum Depression.

56. Depression in general.

57. Post-Pregnancy baby fat and stretch marks.

58. Natural child birth.

59. I am a woman, therefore I want lots of kids.

60. I am a woman, so I hate to be alone.

61. Blonde Bombshell stereotypes.

62. I am just something to have sex with; I have no thoughts or feelings.

63. When I put my jeans in a dryer that's too hot, they shrink up, and when I put them on, I think I've gained weight.

64. When my bosoms are too small to wear a brassiere, but when I wear a white shirt, people tell me I need to wear a bra.

65. There's osteoporosis with my name written all over it.

66. The government wants to tell me what to do with my body.

67. How come at one clothing store, a size six is really a size two, and at another clothing store, a size two is really a size six?

68. Man, I can complain about nothing until the cows come home.

69. Acne when I'm 40. What's up with that?

70. I'm a raging ball of hormones.

71. Explain this one to me: Chin hairs.

72. I weigh less than my man and yet the circumference of my body is still larger than his…Everywhere.

73. I always have to be the sexy one.

74. I hate when a man's boobs are bigger than mine.

75. Why is it that it's erotic and sexual for two or more women to get it on, but when two or more men get it on it's just disgusting?

76. And what's this whole thing about a man being able to orgasm in two minutes, but it takes me forever to climax?

77. This whole menopause deal is outrageous. Why do we have to go through 40 years of cramps, bloating, and hell, just to have about five more years of hot flashes, hormonal changes, and more hell, just so we don't have to bleed anymore?

78. Slow metabolism.

79. I have sex with more than one man, and I'm a slut. A guy has sex with 40 women at once and he's a stud. I'm not buyin' that.

80. ***CRAMPS!!!!*** Good God, the pain!!

81. The uncanny ability to take everything everyone says seriously.

0-595-31892-4

www.ingramcontent.com/pod-product-compliance
Lightning Source LLC
Chambersburg PA
CBHW031327290526
45784CB00014B/2413